learn to draw
Cats & Kittens

Step-by-step instructions for more than 25 favorite feline friends

ILLUSTRATED BY ROBBIN CUDDY

This library edition published in 2016 by Walter Foster Jr.,
an imprint of Quarto Publishing Group USA Inc.
6 Orchard Road, Suite 100
Lake Forest, CA 92630

Distributed in the United States and Canada by
Lerner Publisher Services
241 First Avenue North
Minneapolis, MN 55401 U.S.A.
www.lernerbooks.com

First Library Edition

Library of Congress Cataloging-in-Publication Data

Learn to draw cats & kittens : step-by-step instructions for more than 25 favorite feline friends /
illustrated by Robbin Cuddy. -- First Library Edition.
     pages cm
  ISBN 978-1-939581-66-2
1. Cats in art--Juvenile literature. 2. Kittens in art--Juvenile literature. 3. Drawing--Technique-
-Juvenile literature. I. Cuddy, Robbin, illustrator.
   NC783.8.C36L435 2016
   743.6'9772--dc23
                                                                                        2015007019

9 8 7 6 5 4 3 2

Table of Contents

Tools & Materials

There's more than one way to bring your furry friends to life on paper—you can use crayons, markers, or colored pencils. Just be sure you have plenty of good "cat colors"—black, brown, and white, plus yellow, orange, and red.

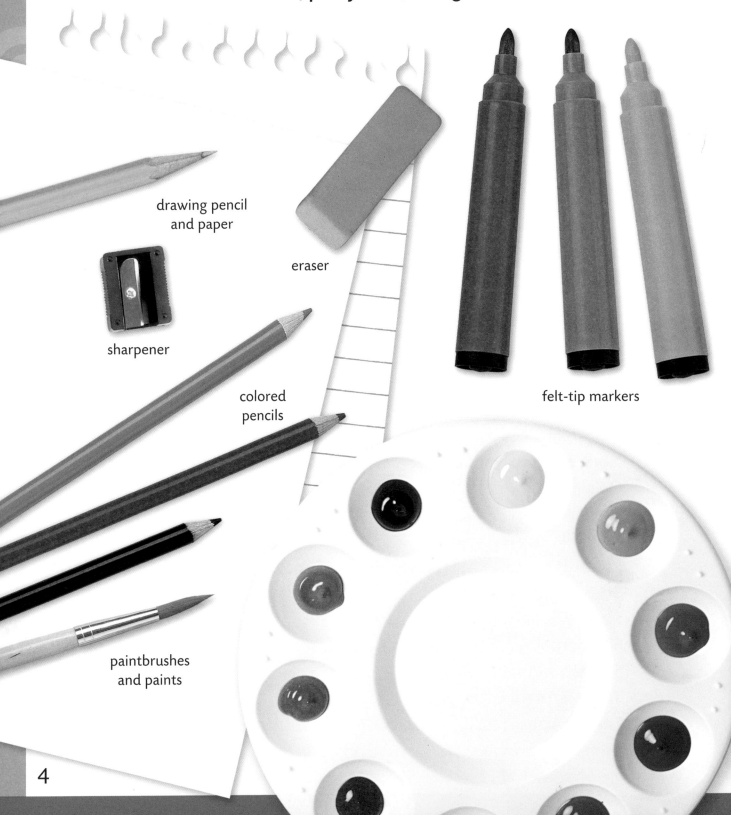

drawing pencil
and paper

eraser

sharpener

colored
pencils

felt-tip markers

paintbrushes
and paints

How to Use This Book

The drawings in this book are made up of basic shapes, such as circles, triangles, and rectangles. Practice drawing the shapes below.

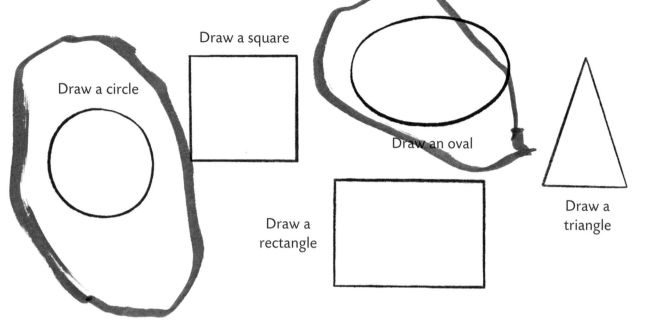

Draw a circle

Draw a square

Draw an oval

Draw a rectangle

Draw a triangle

Notice how these drawings begin with basic shapes.

In this book, you'll learn about the size, origin, and appearance of each featured cat breed. Look for mini quizzes along the way to learn new and interesting facts!

Look for this symbol, and check your answers on page 64!

Breeds

There are about 50 different cat breeds!
Although there are many breeds, most cats fit into one
of the following body shapes: Persian, British Shorthair,
Burmese, and Siamese. The shape of a cat's body typically
indicates which group it belongs to.

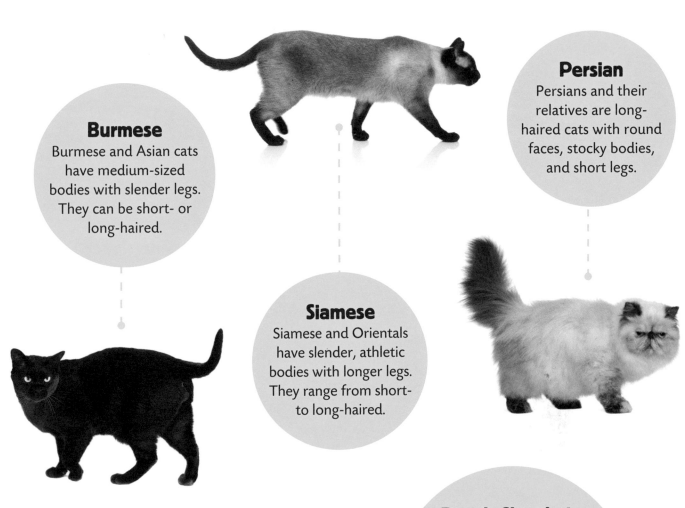

Burmese

Burmese and Asian cats
have medium-sized
bodies with slender legs.
They can be short- or
long-haired.

Persian

Persians and their
relatives are long-
haired cats with round
faces, stocky bodies,
and short legs.

Siamese

Siamese and Orientals
have slender, athletic
bodies with longer legs.
They range from short-
to long-haired.

British Shorthair

British, American, and
European Shorthairs' bodies
are very similar to that of
the Persian. Their bodies are
low to the ground and stocky
like Persians, and they have
round faces and features, but
they are short-haired.

Coats

Coat length varies across breeds and depending on the season.
All cats tend to shed more hair during the warmer months of the year.
Some cats have denser or plusher fur and a double or triple coat.
The undercoat refers to the soft fur closest to the body.

Short-haired Cats

Short-haired cats vary widely in appearance and fur texture, from soft and fine to crimp, curly, and coarse to dense and crisp. It's easier to see the body shape of these cats more clearly.

Hairless Cats

The Sphynx is the only cat breed that is hairless, due to a genetic mutation. The breed was developed through selective breeding and has grown in popularity in recent years. Although it is referred to as "hairless," the Sphynx does have a very fine covering of fur, especially on the ears, face, feet, and tail.

Long-haired Cats

Long-haired cats require a lot more grooming and maintenance than short-haired cats. They tend to shed a lot of their fur in the summer, causing them to look significantly smaller. Persians have the longest and densest fur of all cat breeds.

Abyssinian

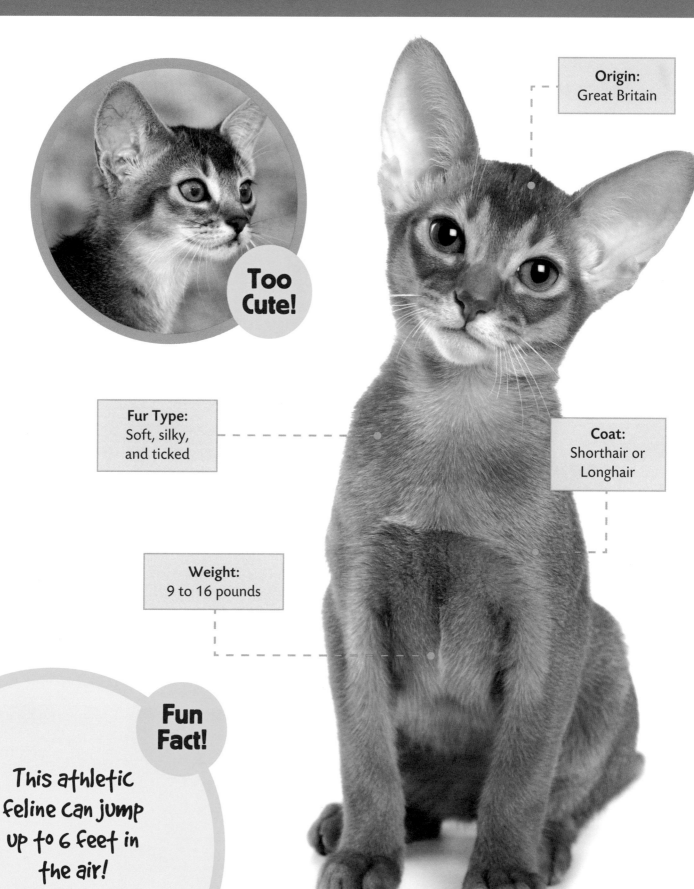

Too Cute!

Origin:
Great Britain

Fur Type:
Soft, silky,
and ticked

Coat:
Shorthair or
Longhair

Weight:
9 to 16 pounds

Fun
Fact!

This athletic
feline can jump
up to 6 feet in
the air!

This lean, muscular breed is very intelligent, loves interacting with humans, and can be taught tricks and trained in obedience.

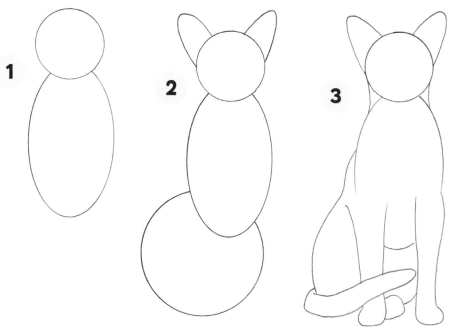

1

2

3

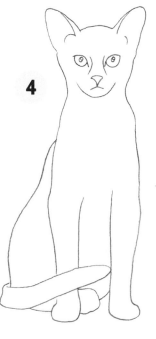

4

5

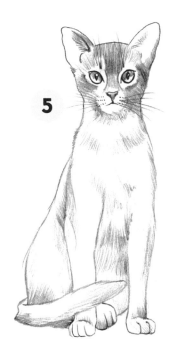

6

Abys' thick, short-haired coats require very little brushing, and they rarely need baths.

Did You Know?

Pet Personality
- Active
- Talkative
- Good with children and other pets

American Curl

Too Cute!

Origin:
USA

Fur Type:
Short and silky;
thin undercoat

Coat:
Shorthair or
Longhair

Weight:
7 to 10 pounds

Discovered in California in 1981, this unique breed is known for its distinct curled ears and playful, affectionate nature.

1

2

3

Mini Quiz

True or false: American curl kittens are born with straight ears.

(Answer on page 64)

4

5

6

11

Balinese

There are two types of Balinese: Traditional, which has a coat more than two inches long, and Contemporary, which has a much shorter coat.

Did You Know?

Weight:
8 to 14 pounds

Fur Type:
Long, fine, and silky

Coat:
Shorthair or Longhair

Origin:
USA

The Balinese enjoys being in high places and is thought to be a less vocal descendent of the Siamese.

Pet Personality
- Intelligent
- Curious
- Loving

1

2

3

4

5

6

13

Bengal

Bengals love to play in water!

Fun Fact!

Fur Type:
Dense, soft, and silky

Coat:
Shorthair

Weight:
10 to 15 pounds

Origin:
USA

These highly intelligent cats are active and
agile and demand a lot of attention.

Pet Personality
• Vocal
• Intelligent
• Playful

Birman

Origin:
Burma
(Myanmar)

Too Cute!

Fur Type:
Long and silky

Coat:
Longhair

Weight:
8 to 12 pounds

Fun Fact!

Birmans lack
an undercoat.

The Birman enjoys the company of people and other pets and prefers to be near the ground rather than on high perches.

Did You Know? All Birman kittens are born completely white—their markings start to appear within the first two years.

Pet Personality
• Sweet
• Gentle
• Social

Bombay

Did You Know?

Bombays are very active and love to play, so they require a lot of attention.

Origin: USA
Coat: Shorthair or Longhair
Fur Type: Shiny, short, and sleek
Weight: 6 to 11 pounds

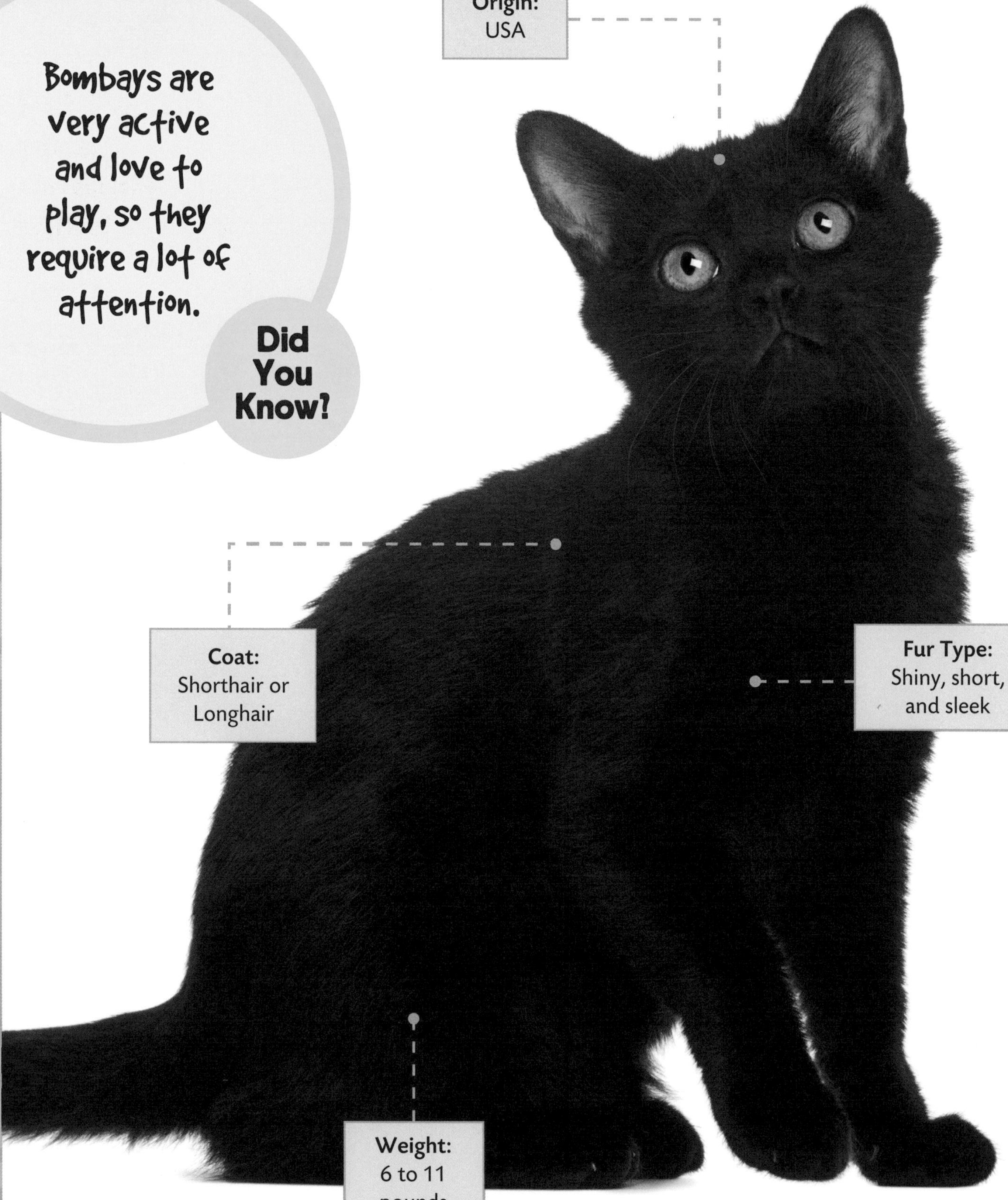

This playful breed has a panther-like appearance and enjoys cuddling and getting lots of attention.

1

2

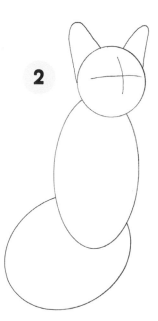

3

Mini Quiz

The Bombay's coat can be which of the following colors?
A. Black
B. Blue
C. White
D. All of the above

(Answer on page 64)

4

5

6

Pet Personality
• Social
• Active
• Affectionate

British Shorthair

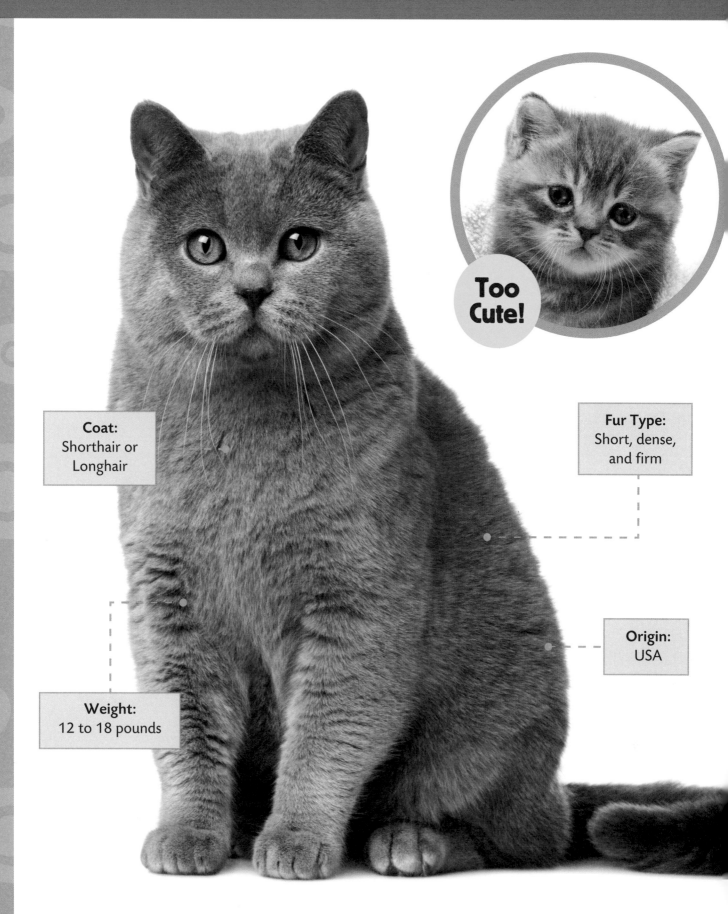

Too Cute!

Coat:
Shorthair or
Longhair

Fur Type:
Short, dense,
and firm

Origin:
USA

Weight:
12 to 18 pounds

This sweet, trusting lap cat loves affection and is very low energy.

1

2

Mini Quiz

True or false: The British Shorthair's coat has more fur per square inch than any other cat breed.

(Answer on page 64)

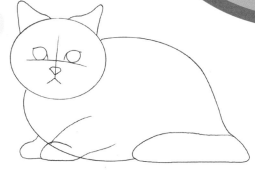

3

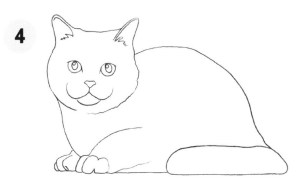

4

5

6

Pet Personality
- Shy
- Affectionate
- Loyal

Burmese

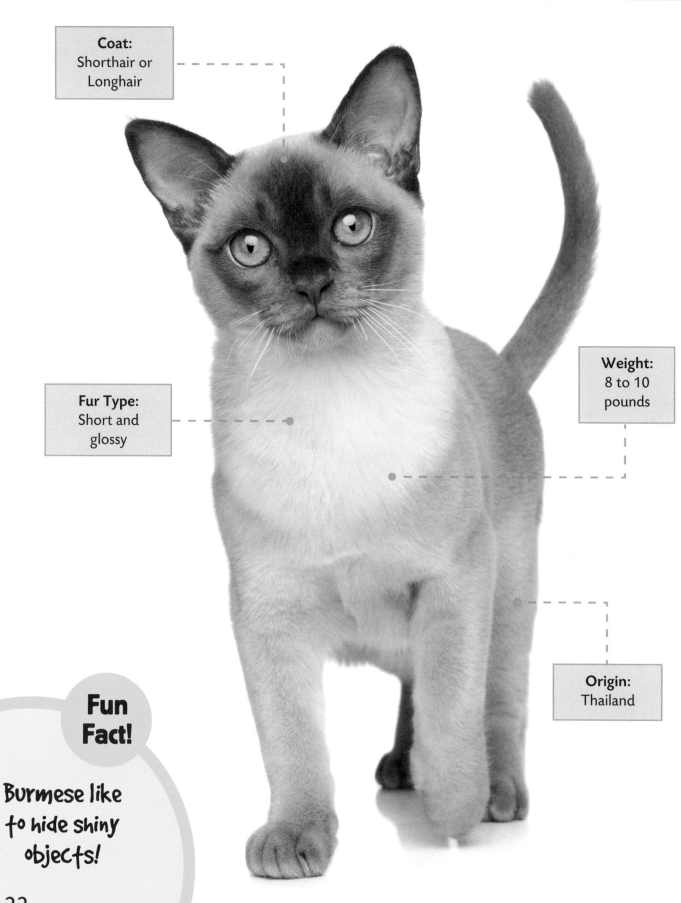

Coat:
Shorthair or
Longhair

Fur Type:
Short and
glossy

Weight:
8 to 10
pounds

Origin:
Thailand

Fun Fact!

Burmese like to hide shiny objects!

This active, muscular breed likes to hang out in high places and requires a lot of mental and physical stimulation.

It's very easy to teach Burmese tricks and how to play fetch—just like dogs!

Did You Know?

Pet Personality
- Social
- Active
- Affectionate

Color Pointed British Shorthair

Color Pointed British Shorthairs are not to be mistaken with Colorpoint Shorthairs, which distinctly resemble the Siamese.

Did You Know?

Weight:
12 to 18 pounds

Fur Type:
Short and dense

Coat:
Shorthair or Longhair

Origin:
Great Britain

Devon Rex

Origin:
Great Britain

The Devon Rex is very smart and loves learning tricks!

Fun Fact!

Coat:
Shorthair or Longhair

Weight:
5 to 10 pounds

Fur Type:
Soft, fine, and curly

This unique-looking breed is known for its short, curly coat
and its wedge-shaped head and large ears.

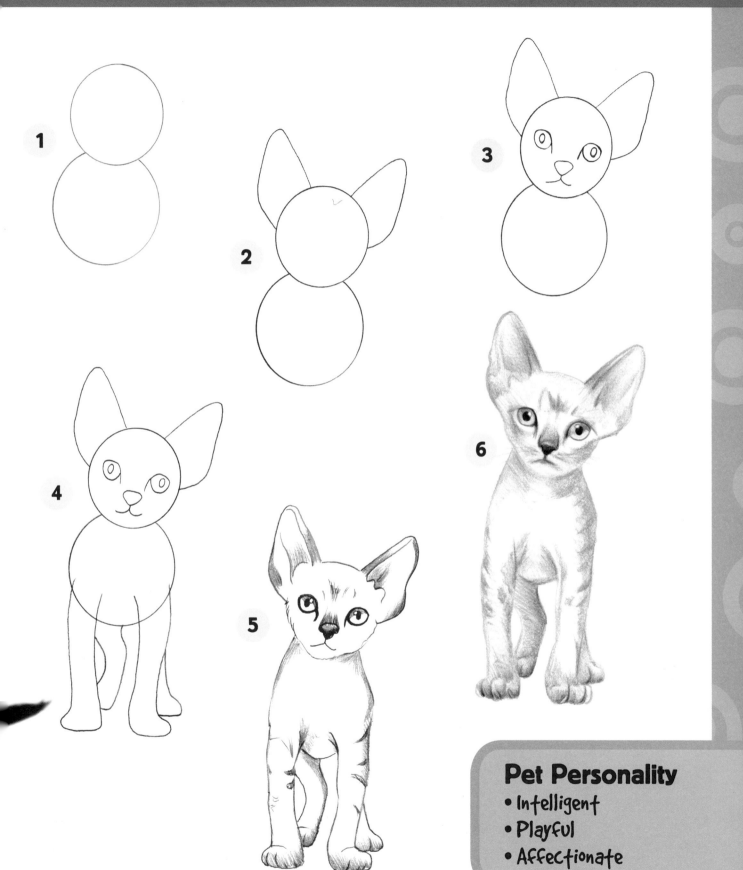

1

2

3

4

5

6

Pet Personality
- Intelligent
- Playful
- Affectionate

Egyptian Mau

Did You Know?

Maus don't get along well with other animals—they prefer to be the only pet of the household. They also prefer not to be picked up, although they still like to cuddle.

Origin:
Egypt

Fur Type:
Dense, fine, and silky

Coat:
Shorthair

Weight:
7 to 9 pounds

This breed is recognized for its spotted coat and its striking resemblance to the cats of ancient Egypt.

1

2

3

4

5

6

Mini Quiz

How fast can Maus run?
A. 15 miles per hour
B. 20 miles per hour
C. 30 miles per hour
D. 40 miles per hour
(Answer on page 64)

Fun Fact!

This athletic, agile breed can jump up to 6 feet in the air from a standing position!

Exotic

Too Cute!

Origin:
USA

Coat:
Shorthair or
Longhair

Weight:
7.5 to 13 pounds

Fun Fact!

This breed does not hit maturity until two years of age.

Fur Type:
Plush and soft

This unique breed looks like a Persian and has the same temperament, but it has a short, dense coat that is easier to groom.

1

2

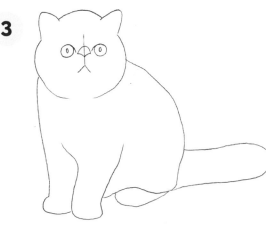

Although Exotics have a gentle, calm personality like their Persian ancestors, they tend to be more friendly and playful.

Did You Know?

3

4

5

Pet Personality
• Quiet
• Affectionate
• Playful

Himalayan

Origin:
USA

Did You Know?

This breed was developed in the 1930s by crossing Siamese cats with Persians.

Weight:
7 to 12 pounds

Fur Type:
Thick, soft, and fine

Coat:
Shorthair or Longhair

Himalayans have long, thick coats that need regular bathing and grooming.

Japanese Bobtail

Pet Personality
- Vocal
- Intelligent
- Athletic

Origin:
Japan

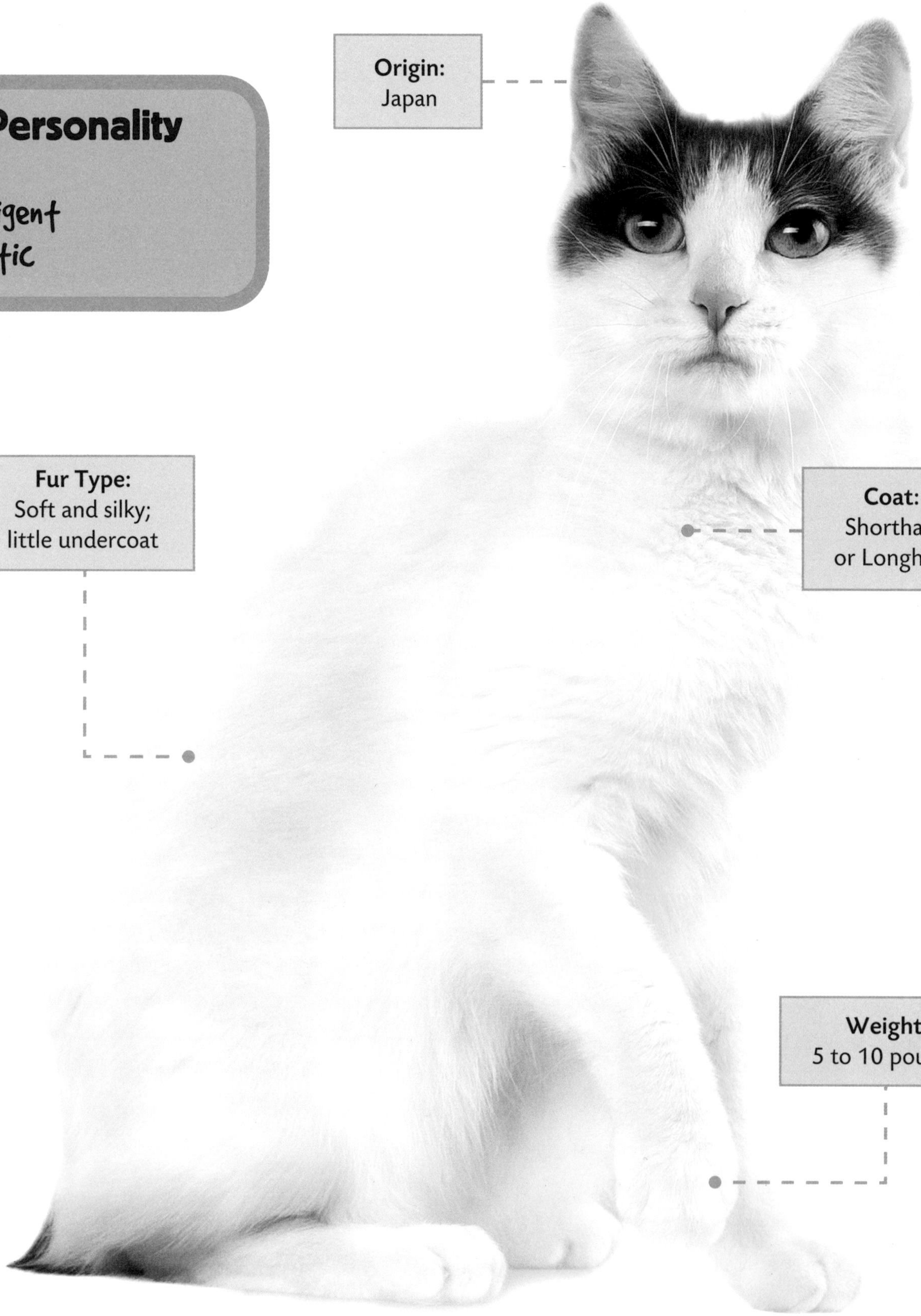

Fur Type:
Soft and silky;
little undercoat

Coat:
Shorthair
or Longhair

Weight:
5 to 10 pounds

The Japanese Bobtail is known for its short, stubby tail.

1

2

3

4

5

6

Japanese Bobtails like to play in water and can be easily trained to perform basic tricks and walk on leashes.

Did You Know?

Maine Coon

Too Cute!

Origin:
USA

Coat:
Shorthair
or Longhair

Fur Type:
Thick and silky

Weight:
8 to 20 pounds

Fun Fact!

Maine Coons can use their front paws to scoop up food and open doors!

This large breed has a shaggy, waterproof coat and a dog-like friendliness.

Mini Quiz

Which of the following are nicknames for the Maine Coon?
A. Shags
B. Gentle Giant
C. American Longhair
D. All of the above

(Answer on page 64)

37

Manx

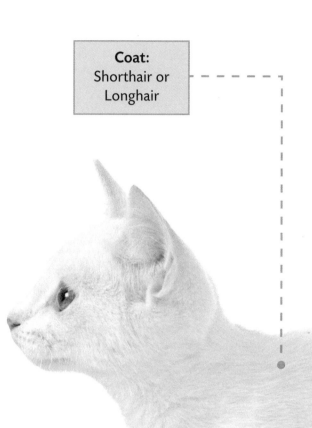

Coat:
Shorthair or
Longhair

Did You Know?

The Manx has one of the shortest torsos of any cat breed.

Weight:
8 to 12
pounds

Fur Type:
Thick undercoat and
longer topcoat

Origin:
Great
Britain

The Manx has powerful, stocky legs and loves to play fetch.

Manx cats like to be in high places, usually on top of shelves or doors.

Fun Fact!

Munchkin

Too Cute!

Coat:
Shorthair or
Longhair

Fur Type:
Medium-
plush and silky

Origin:
USA

Weight:
5 to 9 pounds

Although Munchkins have short legs, they are still very active cats that can jump up on furniture and reach high places.

Pet Personality
- Social
- Playful
- Intelligent

Did You Know?

The Munchkin's short legs are the result of a recessive gene; the rest of its body retains normal cat proportions.

Norwegian Forest Cat

Too Cute!

Origin: Norway

Coat: Shorthair or Longhair

Fur Type: Glossy topcoat and woolly undercoat

Weight: 7 to 20 pounds

Originating in Norway, this breed has a long, waterproof, double-layered coat to keep it warm in freezing temperatures.

1

2

3

4

5

6

Mini Quiz

What color are a Norwegian Forest cat's eyes?
A. Green
B. Gold
C. Copper
D. All of the above

(Answer on page 64)

Pet Personality
• Affectionate
• Gentle
• Patient

Ocicat

The first ocicat was a mixture of Abyssinian and Siamese.

Did You Know?

Origin:
USA

Fur Type:
Short, soft, and shiny

Coat:
Shorthair

Weight:
5.5 to 14 pounds

This wild-looking cat has a sweet, gentle temperament and loves the company of people—family and strangers alike!

Pet Personality
- Social
- Vocal
- Athletic

Persian

Origin:
Persia
(Iran)

Did You Know? This long-haired cat needs to be groomed on a weekly basis so that its fur does not become matted.

Weight:
7 to 10
pounds

Coat:
Shorthair or
Longhair

Fur Type:
Long and silky

This affectionate breed needs attention and enjoys curling up on a favorite human's lap.

Fun Fact!

Long-haired Persians were first discovered in the Middle East in the early 1600s! They were eventually brought to Europe and became very popular in England in the 19th century.

Ragdoll

Origin:
USA

Weight:
9 to 19 pounds

Fun Fact!

This breed is known to love water, so don't be surprised if your Ragdoll joins you in the shower!

Fur Type:
Silky and dense

Coat:
Longhair

Ragdolls are sweet and trusting and, therefore, should never be allowed outdoors without supervision.

Did You Know?

This breed got its name because they often go completely limp when picked up— just like a rag doll.

Pet Personality
- Docile
- Quiet
- Trusting

Scottish Fold

Too Cute!

Coat:
Shorthair
or Longhair

Fur Type:
Dense and
resilient

Weight:
5.5 to 13
pounds

Origin:
Scotland

This affectionate breed is known for its folded ears, which give it an owl-like appearance.

1

2

3

Mini Quiz

How often should the Scottish fold's ears be cleaned?
A. once a month
B. Twice a month
C. Weekly
D. Daily
(Answer on page 64)

4

5

6

Fun Fact! This breed has a tendency to fall asleep while flopped on its back.

Selkirk Rex

Origin:
USA

Pet Personality
• Social
• Laid-back
• Affectionate

Weight:
6 to 16 pounds

Fur Type:
Thick, plush, and curly

Coat:
Shorthair or Longhair

The Selkirk Rex is very mellow and playful and loves to be with people.

Did You Know?

Because of their social nature, Selkirk Rexes should not be left alone for long periods of time.

Siamese

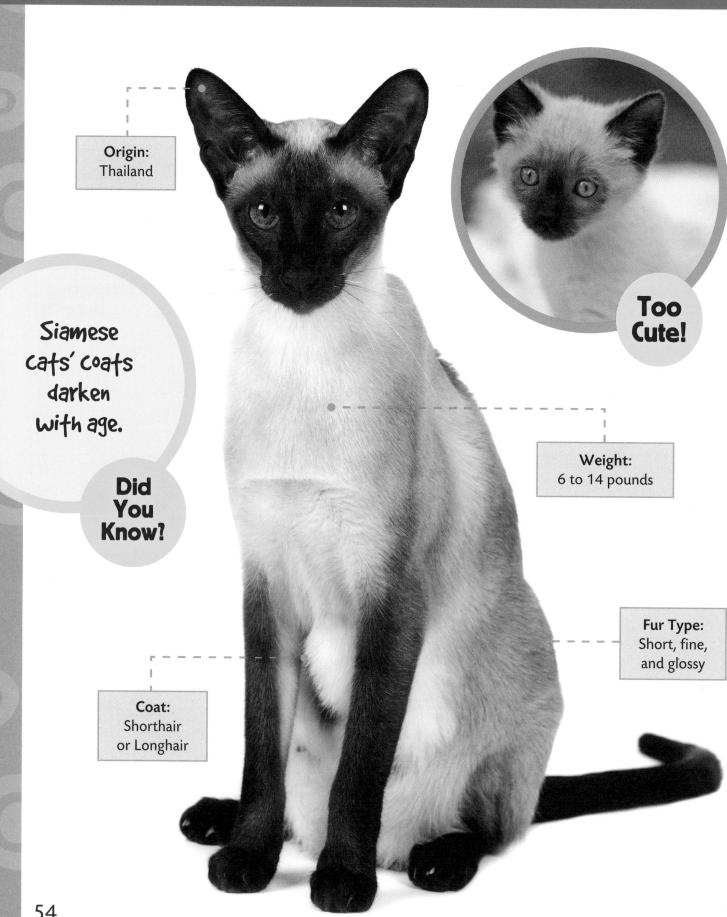

Origin:
Thailand

Too
Cute!

Siamese
cats' coats
darken
with age.

Did
You
Know?

Weight:
6 to 14 pounds

Fur Type:
Short, fine,
and glossy

Coat:
Shorthair
or Longhair

Siamese are extremely talkative cats, and their meows sometimes sound like a crying child.

1

2

3

4

5

6

Mini Quiz

How far back can the Siamese trace its ancestors?
A. 13th century
B. 14th century
C. 15th century
D. 16th century
(Answer on page 64)

Pet Personality
• Very vocal
• Intelligent
• Energetic

Siberian

Too Cute!

Origin: Russia

Fur Type: Glossy topcoat and dense undercoat

Weight: 10 to 20 pounds

Coat: Longhair

This gentle giant is devoted to its owners and good with children.

The Siberian's coat thickens in the winter and sheds in the fall and spring.

Did You Know?

Somali

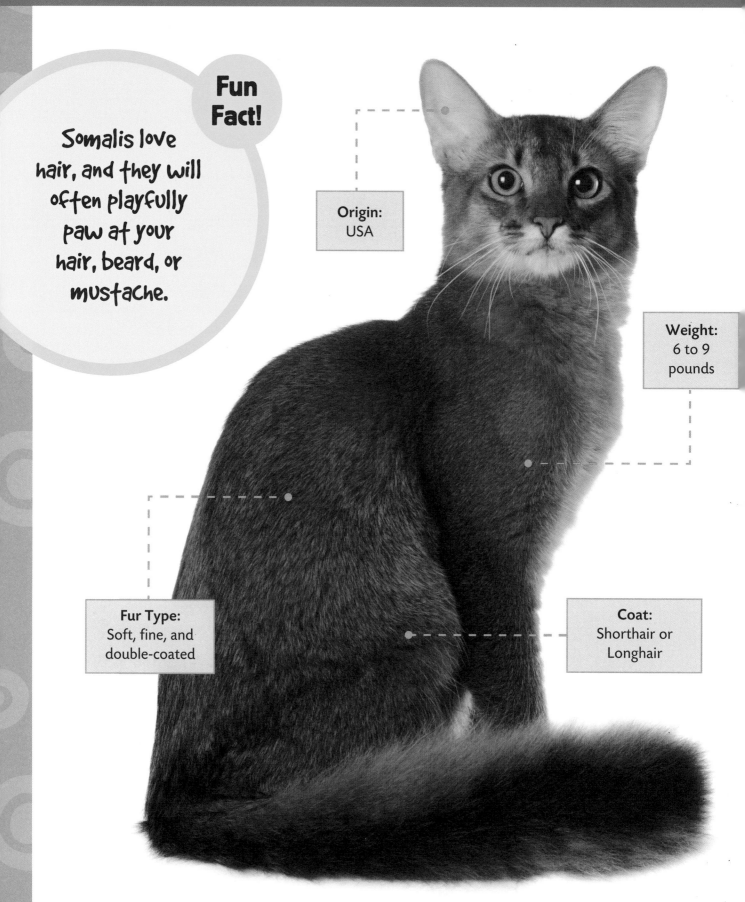

Fun Fact!

Somalis love hair, and they will often playfully paw at your hair, beard, or mustache.

Origin:
USA

Weight:
6 to 9 pounds

Fur Type:
Soft, fine, and double-coated

Coat:
Shorthair or Longhair

This sometimes-mischievous breed is very intelligent and can be trained just like a dog.

1

2

3

4

5

6

Mini Quiz

The Somali is also known as which of the following?
A. Fox Cat
B. Little Lion
C. Biscuit Maker
D. None of the above
(Answer on page 64)

Pet Personality
• Loyal
• Athletic
• Curious

Turkish Angora

Origin:
Turkey

Weight:
6.5 to 18.5 pounds

Coat:
Longhair

Fur Type:
Fine and silky

60

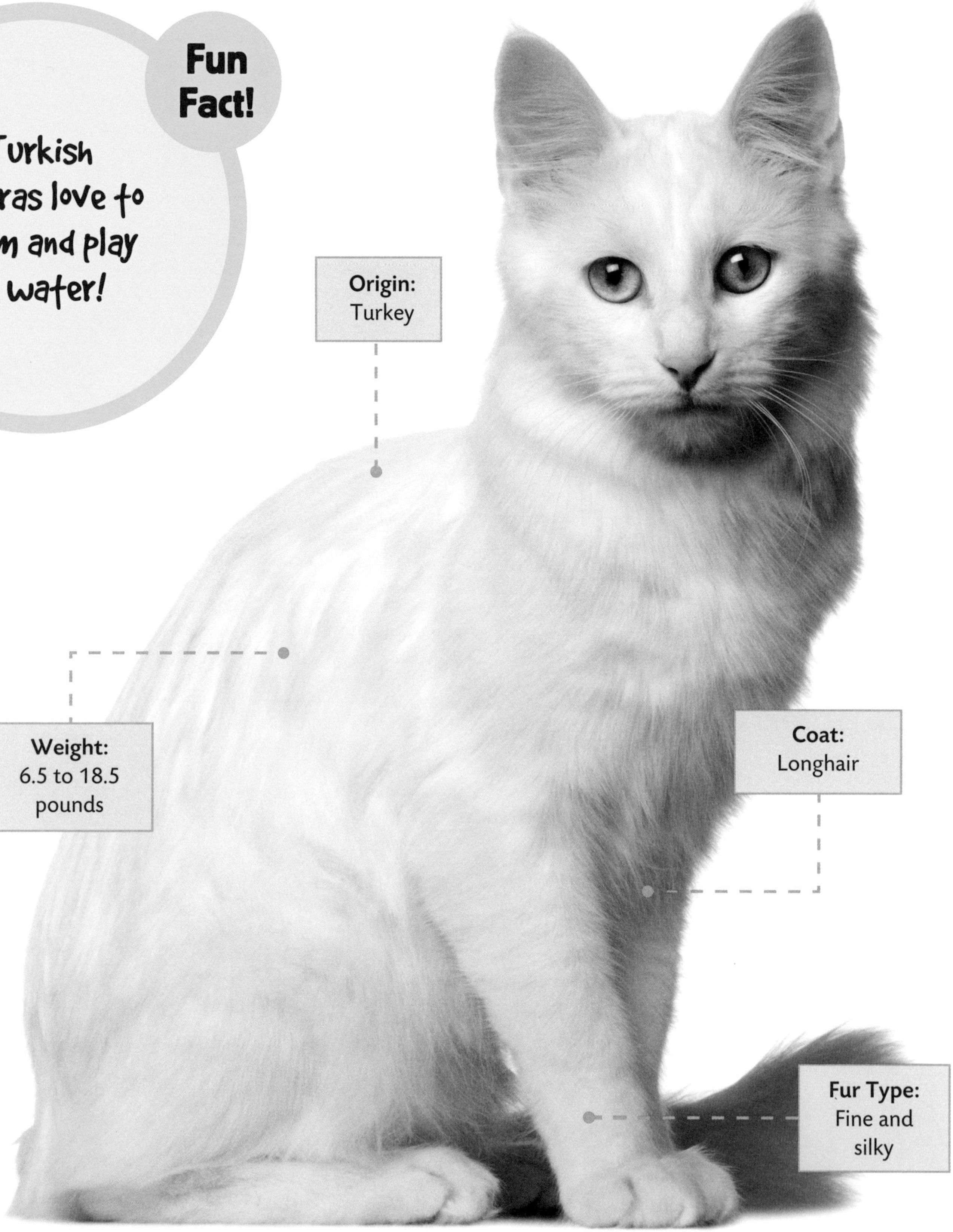

Most Turkish Angoras are known for their long, majestic white fur and having one blue eye and one amber eye.

Did You Know?

Turkish Angoras with one blue eye and one amber eye are usually deaf on the side of the blue eye. Cats with two blue eyes are prone to complete deafness.

Turkish Van

This extremely quick and agile breed is known as the "swimming cat."

Origin:
Turkey

Fur Type:
Soft and silky

Weight:
6.5 to 18.5 pounds

Coat:
Longhair

Pet Personality
• Inquisitive
• Athletic
• Healthy

Turkish Vans enjoy playing fetch and learn obedience commands and tricks easily.

Did You Know?

This breed loves attention from its favorite people, but it does not like to be held.

Mini Quiz Answers

Page 11: True. Their ears begin to curl back within a week after birth.

Page 19: A. Bombays have short, sleek coats that are only black.

Page 21: True. This breed's coat is dense and plush, allowing it to keep warm in cold temperatures.

Page 29: C. Known as the greyhounds of the cat world, Maus can run up to 30 miles per hour!

Page 37: D. Maine Coons are referred to as shags, gentle giants, and American Longhairs.

Page 43: D. Norwegian forest cats can have green, gold, or copper eyes.

Page 51: B. The Scottish fold's ears should be cleaned regularly to remove wax and dirt buildup.

Page 55: B. The Siamese traces its royal roots all the way back to the 14th century in Thailand, when it was called Siam.

Page 59: A. Because of its bushy tail, the Somali has been given the nickname "fox cat."